Hope is a blind bard
Take him in.

For Sister Ruth
love and gratitude
Maura

HOPE
IS A
BLIND BARD

Sister Maura Eichner

Harold Shaw Publishers
Wheaton, Illinois

The *Wheaton Literary Series*

Cover © 1989 by Robert Cushman Hayes

ISBN 0-87788-346-7

Library of Congress Cataloging-in-Publication Data

Eichner, Maura.
    Hope is a blind bard / Maura Eichner.
      p. cm.
    ISBN 0-87788-346-7
    I. Title.
    PS3555.I227H67 1989
    811'.54—dc19   88-28729
                                  CIP

98   97   96   95   94   93   92   91   90   89

10   9   8   7   6   5   4   3   2   1

for family and friends,
sisters and students—
with gratitude

Contents

Part four   **Coming home to light**

Foreword

The radical empiricism of the poet—the ability to see things intensely—is the mark of these poems by Sister Maura: that and the virtue of hope, which feeds her seeing and is fed by it. Describing black-eyed susans, she notes their brilliant petals, their "purple-black, cone-shaped discs," hairy leaves, and thick stems, and agrees with Whitman that "every cubic inch of space is a miracle."

This last statement is the product of no glib wonder or easy ecstasy. It is the hard-won insight of a vision still linked to hope in a world beset by hurricanes and more conscious forces of destruction. The two, vision and hope, fuse together in the following metaphor from "Message from Inland,"

> I have lashed
> a riding
> light
> to my heart,

which provides us with an emblem of the poet's attitude throughout these poems.

Her capacity to hope as well as to see intensely means that she can look steadily at pain, injustice, and suffering. Whether it is a Guatemalan burying his child (dead of poverty) or an inlaw's death by cancer, she finds much evidence of the fallen condition of the race:

> The desperate
> sacrament—man
> conniving with

his own decay.
("iii/Toward an Undefinitive Life of Flannery O'Connor")

The mature faith reflected in these poems enables the poet to
embrace both poles of human experience.

The author is master of a number of forms, from the sonnet to
free verse that, while compressed and trim, is sensuous and musical:

No fragrance
of kelp stirs,
no wind
of sea-change.

Red mud slips
like a secret
beneath
my feet.
("Message from Inland")

In addition to rich, immediate imagery, she can make a poem from
wise observations distilled over a lifetime, the best sort of gnomic
utterance:

A bird in the hand
is not to be desired.

In writing, nothing
is too much trouble.

. . . Make routine
a stimulus. Remember

it can cease. . . .

Hammer on doors with the heart.
("What My Teachers Taught Me I Try to Teach My Students")

Not limited to the lyrical I, Sister Maura writes in a number of
voices—that of Antigone's sister, Ismene, a Disciple's, Thomas
Jefferson's—revealing a fine dramatic sense. Her historical
imagination is joined to an awareness of the social injustices of our
time. With moving plainness she weaves a refrain of the names of
four women martyred in Central America:

Herod ordered the killing.
Shoot them with their hands open
to give hope to the helpless.
Ita, Dorothy, Jean, Maura.
("Central America: Footnote on Social History")

Such lines disturb our complacency about the problems of our
world and the human condition.

But it is finally her visionary presentation of the ordinary that
registers most strongly with the reader. A "Back Porch
Fundamentalist" stares at a mimosa,

where gold wires
of light tapped
the leaves, and he, himself,
by a simple act of seeing

observed a miracle.
If anything is, he said,
them pods
on this tree is the keys
of the kingdom.

Again the poet moves into the object and beyond it as she
meditates upon a hummingbird,

    less
than a penny
in weight.

Who lit
this wonder
for my eyes?

How can I speak
of God
except in the presence
of God?
("From A Summer Diary")

Through such visions, we come closest to the heart of Sister
Maura, with its riding light of hope and our own are warmed and
illuminated.

Robert Siegel

Acknowledgments

We gratefully acknowledge the following publications in which Sister Maura's work first appeared:

America for "Fall of a Kingdom," "Visit with Samuel Beckett," "Flesh Made Word"

Antigonish Review for "Ismene," "Moss Garden," "Portents," "Mideast: Summer Tour," "Litany for the Living"

Beyond the Square: a tribute to Elliott Coleman, J.H.U. for "Friendship without End"

The Bible Today for "The Seduction"

Caim for "Processional"

Christian Century for "Back Porch Fundamentalist," "Out of Cana," "Christmas," "Faith"

Christianity & Literature for "In the Suburbs, Kyoto, Japan"

Commonweal for "Accident," "Grief," "Before the Fall of Rain"

Continental Drift for "Saturday Afternoon at the Writers' Colony"

The Cresset for "Message from Inland," "Adjustment," "Psalm from the Hemoglobin Ward," "The Sign of Mark," "After the El Greco Exhibit," "Writing Class: Senior Citizens," "The Father," "A Remembrance," "What My Teachers Taught Me," "Spring Snow on Long Island," "New York: Lower East Side," "Visit to a T.V. Studio," "Henry Moore in the Five Boroughs," "After Silence"

The Critic for "Toward an Undefinitive Life of Flannery O'Connor"

DES Bulletin for "Last Snow"

Fiddlehead for "Detail for a Summer Afternoon," "Instructions for the Passersby"

Four Quarters for "Medea Mourns Briefly for Orpheus," "Dream Songs Concluded"

Garfield Lake Review for "Aristocrats"

Gathering Voices, anthology for "Visit of Diplomacy: Central America"

Irish America for "Ireland: A Selective Memory"

The Lyric for "Thomas Jefferson at Seventy"

Maryland English Journal for "Morning"

Negro American Literature Forum for "A Woman Is Waiting for a Bus"

New York Times for "Eclogue and Elegy"

Piedmont Literary Review for "From a Summer Diary"

Review for Religious for "Nicodemus"

Sewanee Review for "Imagist at Coney Island"

Sign for "From a Woman's Life"

Sisters Today for "Summer Morning," "Missionaries," "Eucharistic Minister," "Parting," "The Wall Hanging"

Social Issues by Contemporary Poets for "Central America: Footnote on Social History"

South Coast Poetry Journal for "The Physicist Gives Birth to her First Child"

Southern Humanities Review for "Guatemala," "The Coat of Feathers," "Night Walk: Kyoto," "At the Beginning"

Sparrow for "Finding the Body," "From the Book of Commonplace Revelation"

Studia Mystica for "Love Song"

Wascana Review for "Boy in a Museum," "Obituary Note: Lillian Hellman 1905–1984"

PART ONE

A riding light for the heart

Message from Inland

I am clothed
in the seamless
garment
of fog.

No gulls cry.
No nervous horn
sounds
another ship.

No fragrance
of kelp stirs,
no wind
of sea-change.

Red mud slips
like a secret
beneath
my feet.

I know
what happens
to seamless
garments.

I have lashed
a riding
light
to my heart.

Love Song

Past Chancellorsville and Wilderness
battlefields, the blue and gray landscape
where furrows plowed life from dead
slaves, to Louisa County, a little
east of the heart of the heart
of Virginia—to this orchard.

Knuckled wood claws at history.
Wind smooths decay.
Honeysuckle ripens on the barbed
wire fence that walls a ghetto
of apple trees.

Who let it go?—shapeless as heartache?
who turned away from the ripped-off
nest? Which one said—no use,
the fruit's like gall? Who tastes
the guilt?—the fable of us all.

On the Road to Charlottesville

When they came back, with regimental cloth
hanging like rags from wasted bodies,
it was up this road they trudged.

Young master dragged a lantern he had
unhooked from a deserted stable wall.
Sancho bent under winters and a bag

of rot—all the two of them
had clawed from the bereavement
of each day.

Cutting from the road, up this walk
they came, past the sultry meadow,
the pond lined with weeds, the hollow

where a fox had been torn.
There was a bark, and the last
of the golden labradors leaped

from under a broken porch.
A candle hesitated, then took flame.
A door rattled cautiously.

Then they were in a circle of women,
faces in slow grieving motion,
planets around the candle flame.

Later, a grandson of the soldier
set up this stone: To commemorate
seventy five slaves

and especially Sancho Panza
who served his master
1861-1865.

A Woman Is Waiting for a Bus

in the rain, in Baltimore.
Even her big red umbrella
is speechless about courage,
journey's end, the door

of home. Two buses (not
her transfer) pass. She stands
in flooding rain, bulky as
an ark waiting for ararat.

The third bus has come
—gone. She huddles
into rain. Wind sloshes
wetness across her numb

flesh. Open to receive
bitter weather and give back
warmth, she waits—black
ancient beautiful eve.

Still Life: Waiting

Genesis: 18:1-14

The birches are composed
as a Japanese print: mourning
doves move smoothly

through untended grass
around the feeder and the stone
bird bath rooted

like a sun dial in time.

Samantha, the cat,
has wandered away, though someone
continues to fill

her bowl with water.

My brother sits in the shadow
like old Abraham, ready,
hoping that someone will come

with a message different
from the unseen chorus
singing Sophoclean tragedy.

My brother's wife,
skeletal and bald
with the crazed demands

of disease, waits,
sheathed in sheets,
for three angels to come

with promises of life,
wild impossible promises
which will make her laugh

as Sarah did.
She longs to have God
fill his cup

with her laughter.

Mideast: Summer Tour

They remember the driver of the bus,
a tough and gentle Jew.

Long after Tel Aviv, the Lake of Galilee,
the Jordan Valley and Jerusalem,
Bethlehem and Hebron,
when they rode down to Sinai,
braced against washed-out roads,
dieting on dust and heat,
sucking the last saliva to their lips,
before they reached a dig
and excavation shade, he never let
one of them forget the land.

He'd brake the bus: *Look*:
they saw a curving neck lift
lyre horns, a swift gazelle
leap into the dusk; long-eared sheep;
a desert falcon climb the cloudless sky;
red mountainside; granite monastic walls
where, long ago, Moses learned the law.

The driver smiled at them: *Shalom*.
Lightly he dropped his hands
to the submachine gun on his knees.

Visit to a T.V. Studio

Osaka, Japan

The studio is like a hangar:
cameras noosed above
our heads; coils of energy
tubed in rubber underfoot.

We creep through make-believe:
half an ancient train;
rolls of papier-maché street;
tatami stacked like warehouse

cargo; the cardboard
weeping cherry
bending above
the tea house roof;

shadows of leaves brushed
unmoving, on paper windows;
a pile of rock
enormous to the eye

light as incense to the hand.
We watch
actors bow
profoundly to each other

in between
the make-up woman's
hasty mopping
of their brows.

Paper iris bloom;
plastic moss is thick;
plum blossoms
do not fade.

Unseen, the gods
require of us
only our innocence
at the door.

In the Suburbs, Kyoto, Japan

Rice fields edge
open highway.
Intermittent moons
of headlights
glaze still water.

Out of wet marsh
ordered as an abacus,
a harsh harmony of frogs
thrusts at summer air.

We walk the edge
of the paddy,
listening.
From where we were born,
where we have been,
where we are now—
at this moment—
we listen to frogs.

We are enchanted.
The frog is a prince.

Processional

Giacomo Manzu's Monumental Standing Cardinal *was moved by helicopter from Greenwich to the Hirshorn Museum and Sculpture Garden in Washington, D.C.*
Washington Post

He went the way the really big ones go:
a helicopter dropping on the lawn
or swashing down the parking lot, a row
of volks diminishing before the spawn

of noisy winds. And more, he had a cinch
of nylon webbing round his waist, and men
hunchbacked beneath him trying to look up yet inch
the camera lens to catch him close, and then

leap back before 12 feet of bronze spun
uncontrollably beneath the belly cable
of the plane. A Medici would sun
in that! He did. Rose petals blew—unable

to withstand the gust suctioned to his feet,
and men and women gaped him down the street.

Accident

The car was like this:
a crushed corn flake box.

How? they swung off the beltway,
a side road, up an embankment

into the oak. So drunk
they were loose as mud.

So sober they walked out
like the three young men

from the fiery furnace.
You remember their names, don't you?

Fall of a Kingdom

At a banquet
to please his guests

Charlemagne served
one thousand peacocks.

Tearing meat
from bone of breast,

the warriors swallowed,
with the ale,

six feet of bronze
and iris-green,

blazing blue
turret of throats,

all-seeing eyes.
And it was no

dream—the old
servant

sweeping up
stinking rushes

after the feast
saw the evil eye

upon the floor,
skeletons

of war lords
in the open door.

Ismene

Antigone was the brighter
of the two of us.
A shrug-off person,
a little annoyed with fuss

and palace rules. She
was my father's favorite.
Not my mother's. Once
a seer had a fit, or perhaps

a vision at the shrine
in the inner court.
Everyone ran. My sister
stayed. She knew the report

they gave my father. She
touched my mother's jeweled pin.
When I could not look at the pulp
where his eyes had been

she said: you *must* look
and remember. Creon's son
never stopped looking
at her. Finally won

her for bride. That was
before my brother was fed
to ravens, and I sickened
at the overfed

glut of the vultures.
Antigone did not wait
in the cave; she
chose her fate.

Wailing clogs my ears
to this day;
the smell of funeral pyres
never blows away.

I, Ismene, am dead;
I am Creon's ward.
I have a little knife.
I have a cord.

I use neither.
I try. I fail.
Antigone lives forever.
And I tell her tale.

Detail for a Summer Afternoon

The name of the cat is "Mousetrap."
At the moment, he blooms
in a long stone flowerbox
(empty on the porch). There is room
for his grave in it. That is not
his intent. He dozes and grooms
himself: a waking sleep. He is a cat
for Cleopatra's hand to touch:
as cool and hot as that.

Saturday Afternoon at the Writers' Colony

Benignly, a member of the Board
of Trustees came to bless
the writers. He could afford

the luxury of patronage
now—after the stockyard
years. He bent the hedge

of privet quietly hoping to find
a poet like a Keatsian pearl
in the center of a sand-grind

of words. He found—sleeping
near the sunlit stream—the poet
naked as a piece of string.

Instructions for the Passersby

There was, beside the air conditioner and
under the overhanging ledge, a hand's

breadth of stone window sill. Here
the pigeons made a nest: a sphere

of dry grass and weed, flimsy
as rhetoric, grotesquerie

of safe/secure. The male sat, a repose
of rock with a fixed eye, verbose

as stone. The female came at dusk,
nudging herself in place with a brusque

downsweep of wings, bosomy cluck.
Her eyes crowded us, like a truck

clearing the lane. So they sat, he
and she, for five weeks. And we

watched. Under them, two eggs, white
and glossy, warmed by day, by night.

The pigeons, hard as billiard balls,
held us with their look. Lightfalls,

dawnings, never early, never late,
they tamed us: how and why to wait.

Finding the Body

Suddenly the chrome rectangular
cold water fountain balked.

The swollen base leaked
outhouse stench.

Water poured from the mouth-
spout into rising scum.

Savage as Goya we scooped
back-up sewage.

Turn off the water.

Turn off the water.

where?

where?

WHERE?

We bailed water like treads
on the belly of a snake

until someone dumbly keyed
the sodden water pipe

and we dragged away our bodies
bulged like voice sacs of the

wetland frogs or birds with
feathers fouled from oil.

Ladies Asleep on the Greyhound

The ladies adjusted their feet
to the candy paper wrappers on the floor;
clutched their handbags firmly,
and a brown paper bag of snacks.

The ladies unleashed their air-
conditioned bones to the springs
of the seats. Talk ran down—
like water from old faucets.

The ladies pushed back their hair
that was acting unruly, surprised
at being out all night. Gradually
they forgot the hiss of the air-brake.

The ladies slept. Two of the
muses (perhaps?) taking a late vacation—
their garlands, the lyre, the flute
in the dream.

Little Ballad for the Moment

Down came Zaccheus,
branch to branch,
down came Zaccheus
rubbing his calf,
for he hadn't shinned
up a sycamore tree
in more than half
a century.

Down came Zaccheus
planning the meal:
delicious dishes,
herbs to smother
fresh-caught fishes,
warm baked bread,
honey and dates,
wine so red
the fine bouquet
hung in the air
like a young girl's hair.

Down came Zaccheus,
saying: "honest, I
will give it back—
not someday,
but *now*: all that

I cheated and took
by baiting or better—
with a taxman's hook
and a warning, "fail—
and I promise you jail."

Down came Zaccheus,
branch on branch
and Jesus waiting
to give him a chance
to be free.

Coda
Lord, when taxes are
heavy and due (always)
so it seems right now,
and what they call
world-wide inflation
has a time span of
eternal duration,
Lord, between you and me,
call down Zaccheus
from my sycamore tree.

The Library: South Stair

Never use the elevator.
Choose the south stair—up or down.
The heavy door swings behind you
and you are in Poe's Dupin-dusk
climbing past the pock-marked cinder blocks—
each a coffin wide and long.

Walk slowly;
a sorcerer's light, pale mustard yellow
seeps from a narrow skylight.
Hercule Poirot may appear,
head bent a little left,
waxed moustache pointing upward.

Lean over the stairwell, breathe
the air Perry Mason once exhaled
in courtroom oratory.
There is a scarlet wheel
that will unleash a waterfall
should Peter Wimsey command.

Always, before research or scholarship,
walk the south stair.
Detectives clear frustration, guilt,
confusion. Fixed laws
control the universe, and
once you find your carrel in the stacks,
Jane Marple will appear
with a cup of tea.

Grief

Who will go down
to this ocean floor?

this mystery less known
than craters of moon?

who will dive gently
into the sea of tears

on whose shore you stand
nudging my heart

with your careless foot?

The Wall Hanging

Indians, living along Lake Atitlan
weave this cloth out of their life,

their land. Tropical Guatemalan
color—brighter than the quetzel,

that hidden bird, magnificent in plumed
quietness. They recreate an innocent

universe: featureless dog, monkey, duck,
pheasant. If their hearts break,

the shuttle does not. The ripe
designs grow, held in place

by the Eucharist, primal, glowing
in purple and gold.

Guatemala

The cloth strap fitted across his forehead,
twisted into rope above his shoulders.
It held the homemade box
on his back. In it his son lay dead.

Mid-day enlargement of white sun
glazed the box; sweat and held back tears
polarized the father's eyes to the beaten road
from the coffee plantation to the dry dun

of the workers' cemetery. At home, the mother
wailed; the children fumbled uneasily
among chickens and rabbits, uncertain
of the life they saw in each other.

The father stood a long time at the grave
he had dug. He could not bear to lift
the strap from his brow, release the box
from his back. His wet shoulders gave

in at last. He let the coffin into the hole
carefully—as a man puts good seed in earth.

Central America: Footnote on Social History

Peasants found the bodies of four women by a roadside in the village of Santiago Nonualo on Dec. 3, 1980. They were identified as Maryknoll sisters Ita Ford and Maura Clarke, Ursuline nun Dorothy Kazel and lay worker Jean Donovan. They were allegedly raped then shot at close range.
Newsweek, June 4, 1984

Herod ordered the killing.
Shoot them with their hands open
to give hope to the helpless.
Ita, Dorothy, Jean, Maura

It was done. Like felons,
they were hidden in unmarked graves,
scapegoats, caked with blood.
Dorothy, Jean, Maura, Ita

Later, hauled up by ropes
cutting breasts, ankles, wrists, their
loose-hanging heads gaped with gun holes.
Jean, Maura, Ita, Dorothy

Ramah's voice wails and laments.
Unseen, four queenly women waken
our hearts to wonder, freedom, God.
Maura, Ita, Dorothy, Jean.

Visit of Diplomacy: Central America

The wife of a visiting politician
was impressed—riding smoothly

from the Presidential Palace
to a seasonal home on the lush

green mountainside. Everything
was right: Latin-American courtesies;

iridescent birds singing from bush
and tree sheltering the patio-feast;

white-coated Indian waiters serving
deftly. It was later, when she

accidentally lost her party on tour,
that she stood, sick and unclean,

watching waiters scrape the dinner
guests' plates into the hands

of their thin-legged children,
caged like rabbits, their bones

clattering over gristle, crumbling
tacos, darkening banana skins.

PART TWO

The word will have the last word.

Visit with Samuel Beckett

He drank the champagne
convivially, drank for the name
Lachrymae Christi—letting his fingers

taste the stenciled words
as the angle that he poured
stretched like a yawn. He went

to see his play—saying wrong,
all wrong. It should be sung,
it should be salt on the skull,

flame on the truncated edge
of a sword, should be the ridge
of mystery where poems stalk.

Listen to the bruise-colored years,
the penny-whistle noise. Look at the tears.
And silences.

The heart, that stubborn instrument
of love, promises only the blunt:
the word will have the last word.

A Remembrance

of things past: John Berryman
slated to speak in the Mayo Auditorium
and almost every summer session student
vowing to be there.

Packed house: Berryman shuffles
past the lectern and stares.
Silence. He wants *more* of that:
absolute quiet. Absolute thickens
phlegm in dry throats, coughing rattles
the room, notebooks slide, a cigarette
lighter clinks against an arm rest,
breathing is fortissimo. . . .

Absolute silence

After a long time he does not read his poems.
He talks about Anne Frank. He holds her diary
like a host speaks of her presence.

Of that evening, I remember
three thoughts: "Anne," he said,
"disciplined herself to get up each morning
as though hope were at the door.
There has not been so witnessing a word
since Augustine's *Confessions*."

Grace is everywhere.

Dream Songs Concluded

in memory of John Berryman 1914-1972

Henry was sick of winter, John dying of
living. Together they walked across the bridge

to the library. Following truth, no doubt,
John said. Truth detoured,

going home the short way—under water.
John followed like a bulging sack.

Henry turned,
fled back to the printed page.

Under black water truth cored the river.
John sucked the dark totality into his lungs.

Truth absorbed the pull of tide, plunged
into the root of water. John followed,

gained momentum in desire, felt the coldness
of the fire, brilliant burning of the root.

While sirens stopped to let the grappling
nets into the river, someone gave the story

to the press, the pictures to T.V.
"He chose the wrong way."

Not so John said not so. Mercy and truth
are one in the root of the river.

At last I am free.
I am free.

Imagist at Coney Island

One decade into the 20th century,
Pound, with his back

to Brooklyn, pointed his beard
to the Atlantic. Simply

to receive the kingdom, Ezra
linked arms with John Butler Yeats.

Their shoes filled with sand. Pleasure
rode the water, solid as Staten Island Ferry.

At dusk, lights rose like a fever chart,
Coney Island "marvelous against the night."

In the amusement park Yeats
rode an elephant on the merry-go-round,

"smiling Elijah in the beatific vision."
Pound leaned against a railing

pouring sand from each shoe,
words ripening in him in August heat.

Toward an Undefinitive Life of Flannery O'Connor

i

All writers are local somewhere. . . .
Flannery O'Connor

Trace her lineage
to Adam, to Eve

in the garden.
Riddle what she gave,

what understated,
overloaded;

choices imposed,
or choices taken.

These storm the thin woods
of the world.

The smallest leaf is shaken.

ii

The key word is see. . . .
Flannery O'Connor

When her father was young,
and she was a child,

she kept pea fowl
and a chicken that lumbered

like Gammer Gurton.
Later, they remembered

how little she said
while jeremiads slumbered

in her small bobbed head.

iii

The salt of the poem lives on. . . .
Lawrence Durrell

Faulkner
she put aside

as one whose rhythms
would override

her plain tale:
the desperate

sacrament—man
conniving with

his own decay.
She read Conrad

41

and James
whose traces

would not diminish
the Mauriac faces
enduring her truth.

iv

Prophecy is a matter of seeing. . . .
Flannery O'Connor

Honesty, dry
heat,

opened like
a parachute

in the enormous
shadow

of her crutches:
the comic

in the uncanny,
neurotic, demonic—

the human face
I look at

is me.

v

To be humble in the face of what is. . . .
Flannery O'Connor

In the end
she heard the clear-

eyed devil
say: "Friend,

you write *that* crap?"
Then she knew

Ezekiel's vision
totally true;

Old Adam
talked southern;

her brother death had
always been about,

sworn by God
to lift her out

the fiery jewel kiln.

Listening to the Commentary

on the death of Ernest Hemingway
July 2, 1962

i

He was cleaning a gun.
There was no note. He wouldn't care
what they reported. Who can say.
No one was there.

He was a Catholic. Not
any more. When does a man
stop being what he is. He
was a Byron. No, a Mark Twain.

The thing to do is last
and get your work done, he said.
The Sheriff gave the coroner
time for his report. Dead?

ii

Generations not yet born will refute
that word applied to him. He chose
his own order of people to love.
In India, Australia, China, everyone knows

he had the Nobel Prize for
the Old Man. He was free and brave.
And the President mourned.
Burial. It will be like Joyce's grave

a—The picture magazines did well.
He was a drinker, fighter. But now,
after the tempest. Now.
He, too, plucked the golden bough.

Medea Mourns Briefly for Orpheus

Orpheus had sung
the marriage hymn
at their wedding.

Jason listened
though his eyes
never left

the golden fleece.
Under ceremonial boughs
of the island,

Medea herself
had lidded
her eyes

to watch a
settlement of worms
at her sandal toe.

Nevertheless, she
wished now
that the Ciconean

women had not
torn Orpheus to
bleeding shreds

for his scorn of them.
If Orpheus were
alive, he might sing

now, before the nurse
brought Jason's children
to their mother.

If his hand
flamed the lyre
string, he might melt

that smooth round
stone that banged
in her breast

where Apollo's priest
said a human heart
was supposed to be.

Past Is Present

When Queen Hatshesut reigned
in the New Kingdom of the Nile,
she wore amulets jeweled
with inlay of tile

smooth turquoise and red
jasper. Her fingers played
on the lapi lazuli
while a slave's hand stayed

and let the lute string
fragility of sound
from a high-domed carapace
of the turtle found

in the river shallows.
Under museum glass
are amulet and shell.
Staring, the viewers pass:

Queen Hatshesut with
the slave lad — more real
than the weightless
downward reel

through sun god space
when astronauts heard
Oriental music crying
like some experimenting bird.

The Coat of Feathers

The son of the emperor
Hsuan Tsung, wore, over his armor,
a sleeveless coat of feathers.
Across his breastbone, the tremor

of body plumage of the drake;
dark glow of copper pheasant
on his shoulder, and like overhanging
tiles on his back, renascent

green barbs and webs (also from
the pheasant). Striding the palace
in his sleeveless jimbaari, the emperor's
son felt his immortality. Yet Patroclus

having only Homer's song about his
armor lived longer; the son
of Daedelus continues
his flight to the sun. A twine

of hemp covered with feathers
in the Oriental Room, British Museum
seems to be all that remains of
the prince. Enough for a slight poem.

One drop changes the ocean's deep.

The Sign of Mark

"Immediately" is the chosen word of Mark.
He writes: Here begins the great good news
of Jesus Christ, the Son of God; the dark
is pushed aside by light. He who would choose
to come in human flesh would gravely let
himself be baptized. At once, "immediately,"
the Spirit ratified the act. Then Jesus met
the brothers, Simon and Andrew. "Immediately"
they moored their boats and nets to follow Him.
That's how it was: a woman who was ill,
a paralytic man—heart-need, not whim
directed Jesus. Mark breathed in miracles.

Importunate, he dramatized his plea:
Come to the Son of God *immediately*.

The Seduction

John passim

That was his way with us. "Come and see." Or
"Come follow me." We did. And we became
the deepest meaning of those words. They tore
us from familiar things: a home, a name,
our work—these mattered less and less. Why?
That's what we asked ourselves. And that was not
important. What was?
                    Once that man walked by
and called, we followed. Who? And what
came next? Everything. He spoke: earth, sea
obeyed him. What he did, he was. He went
to sinners, ate with them. And suddenly
they changed and were his friends. He prayed. He spent
himself. What more?
                    We found Jesus Christ, he—
the Son of God, here, in Galilee.

Nicodemus

Who is that man? can God both eat and drink?
lift up a child? walk toward a tree for shade?
use spittle to make clay? sleep on a bank
of hay? be warmed by sun? can a man raid
the mystery of mysteries and bring
forgiveness to a world?
Nicodemus came
to question Christ when ruddy lights only hung
where whores were waiting. *Jesus Jesus* the name
stumbled on his lips. *Jesus, tell*
me — how can these things be? Jesus smiled
into the dark. "Man must be born again. Will
you, friend?" *How? How?* "Be open as a child.
Believe. Hope. That is all you need to know.
We will carry each other home the day that we go."

Henry Moore in the Five Boroughs

Great works of sculpture should be part of our everyday lives.
George Ablah on the loan of his Henry Moore Collection to the
City of New York

Summer. The bronzes of Henry Moore,
coal miner's son from Yorkshire,
tell their inexhaustible stories

to a new world of listeners. "Size,
itself," says Moore, "is impact."
As though New Yorkers did not know.

Reclining or seated, his sculpted women,
forms of love have riddles
to expound. Dawn-dew clings

to a falling warrior, the atom
piece, the totem head. Sunlight
stencils flesh-colored shadows

on bronze. One half million eyes (more
or less) inhale the breath
of Henry Moore on the Sheep Meadow,

at the Duck Pond, the Bronx Zoo,
or City Hall. Each finite
angle of vision opens a moment

of light, reality, presence. Wildly,
the leaves charade applause.

Obituary Note: Lillian Hellman 1905-1984

The Times gave her an obit page. "Miss Hellman
left no survivors." Other facts: dates:

birth, death, plays, early, late.
Dashiell Hammett; the Fifth Amendment;

An Unfinished Woman, etc. etc.
And I . . . for half my lifetime, have watched

years runneling down her face;
listened to her draining search

for truth: trenchant, prophetic,
compassionate. I have left her theatre

resurrected from the world's sorrow
for a moment, holding fish and honey-

comb in my hand. Say what you will,
facts lie. She has survivors.

Aristocrats

Freaks were born with their trauma.
They're aristocrats.
Diane Arbus

They do not dread
the bestial experience.

They seem to
hang to life

like a huddle
of onions drying

on the side of
a barn. But no—

they pass the test:
they touch the place

of beginning like
eastern musicians

drumming the sun down.

On Rereading Augustine

Who had sung the song
he did not know: *tolle lege*
take and read . . . *take.* . . .
Life crowded Augustine:
wildness, sex, passionate
needs, festering pears.

Leaves stirred, a bird sang
on the garden wall: *take*
and read . . . the sing-song
of a child. Augustine wept,
picked up Paul's letter
and read: Make Christ
your armor.

Who had sung that song?
Who sings to you? to me?
Before I dare to say
I do not know, I hear, once more,
the many-voiced bird
singing in the cage
of my reality.

Waiting

I walk through silence.
A Red Sea parts straight
before me, closes again
over the chariots of sound.
I wait.

On red mud, I walk
unpracticed, unadept. Late
in learning, my heart is a Miro
bell, one side without a shell.
I wait.

I tell myself: be ready
to be unready. Sate
yourself with nothing; want
nothing more than that.
And wait.

I am a climber up far
enough to see air vibrate
beneath me rather than
above. I only know enough to
know: wait.

New York: Lower East Side

Sally Fitzgerald lectures on Flannery O'Connor

Outside the Catholic Worker
House on East Third,
the street quiets.
Panhandlers huddle
in stair wells, winos hunker
over heat grids, pushers
chart the alleys,
bag ladies rummage life
from lifeless matter.

Inside, to a Friday night
gathering, someone talks about
Flannery O'Connor
who never was
like anyone else.

Flannery did not misjudge
the ultimate resurrection
of the freak-prophet.
She knew grace triumphed
on the moon-crusted empire
of the devil; that,
terrified, man is free
to become more human.

Listeners pull toward
the speaker, sit hard
on wooden chairs, staring

beyond the dark windows
where grace pours down,
as always, violent.

Three from Thoreau

i

Song of the Wood Thrush

"Whenever a man hears
it, he is young. . . ."
He forgets his fears.
Whenever a man hears
it, he smiles; his tears
become lyrics to be sung.
"Whenever a man hears
it, he is young. . . ."

ii

Two Wood Thrushes Flew into the Forsythia

When a wood thrush came this spring,
another followed: the song was true.
Yellow forsythia seemed to sing
when a wood thrush came this spring;
the bush was alive as a wedding ring:
one perfect song rounded from two.
When a wood thrush came this spring,
another followed. The song was true.

Take Thoreau's Word for It

"Whenever a man hears a thrush,
it is a new world," says Thoreau.
No matter the haste, the rush,
whenever a man hears a thrush,
spring comes with dogwood flush.
Someone said it who ought to know:
"Whenever a man hears a thrush,
it is a new world," says Thoreau.

What My Teachers Taught Me
I Try to Teach My Students

A bird in the hand
is not to be desired.

In writing, nothing
is too much trouble.

Culture is nourished, not
by fact, but by myth.

Continually think of those
who were truly great

who in their lives fought
for life, who wore

at their hearts, the fire's
center. Feel the meanings

the words hide. Make routine
a stimulus. Remember

it can cease. Forge
hosannahs from doubt.

Hammer on doors with the heart.
All occasions invite God's

mercies and all times
are his seasons.

PART THREE

Hope is a blind bard.

Before the Fall of Rain

The cat cries. A young goat
whimpers for a human step
beside his own gavotte.
Magnolias stretch umbrella
leaves; a toadstool changes
to an ikon in the sagging air.

Under shrubs of box,
stone and root—like hedge-
schoolmasters—hoarsely whisper:
hope is a blind bard.
Take him in.

Winter

Power lines
locked in ice
fall into cold seas
of suburban lawns.

Unseen sun shines
on ice-cased shrubs
riding like breakers
to the storm door.

On the back porch,
navigators search
for daylight stars
above glass oceans.

The Child

He created a world.
Yours. Mine. Shall we ever
explore it?

His fingers curled
on yours, mine, sever
our hold on everything

else. Will he—
live? We are uncertain,
in a dark:

a centered fluidity,
an albumen planet.
Out of your seed

in me, he *is*.
And he has made us
a people

totally his.
We are almost ready
for God.

Flesh Made Word

It is hard,
Beckett says,
to accept the light.
"God is love.
Yes or no?
No."

    And yet
this thirst
for infinity.
Nothing satisfies.
Everything falls
short.

    Then,
ready or not,
this child comes,
reading his mother's eyes,
needing her breast.

But only a child,
mind you,
flesh that could
hang from a nail
from horny wood.

Why, in the night,
should we reel
from the shock
of that presence?

find in our doubt
and sweat
this astonishing hope?

Morning

A few oak
and sycamore
shadows
float quietly
in water.
The sun
like a master
of candlelight
pierces city haze.
Around the reservoir
the joggers
tlot tlot
through an
outcry of
gnats
tlot tlot
an exhaustion
of weeds
tlot tlot
on the mesmerizing
circle of
Poseidon's
city pond—
men
stalking
their future,
blunting
the paunch
of Bacchus.

How Tom Sawyer, etc.

The boy has a summer job:
on the muddy shore
of the library lagoon
he wields a seven foot pole
with a net (he is four
feet—standing high).

He sweeps the net
into thick-scummed water:
salvaging beer cans, plastic
lotion bottles, McDonald's
cups, pizza platters. He bags
debris like Aeolus
keeping his winds.

Then the kids come with their dog.
They reconnoiter. Finally *Let
me Let me.* Ecstatic, the dog
slithers in mud, showering them all.

Thoughtfully, the boy hands over
the net. It is heavy. They recoil
from Newton's Law. Try again. Again.
The boy watches their arms ache,
pontificates—pack the trash
carefully.

Later, he sits above the silt
whistling an off-key tune
of the entrepreneur.

Portents

Two o'clock:
a fanged wind
hurtles garbage cans;

deliberately,
a spectacular
cardinal

plucks scarlet
from leafless
branches.

I scrape
pigeon droppings
from the kitchen

window. Snow
is coming
whining like a dog.

From the Book of Commonplace Revelation

Uneasy afternoon:
tea-colored sky

silence waiting
for a tornado.

You and I
rode home like

women expecting
a drug field

at the turn
of the stair.

Instead—rain
piercing as nails

or bricks
facing a heart,

water hissing
like whetstone

on a knife—
grinder's wheel.

Ah—
suddenly

across housetops
and trees

the noiseless
explosion

of sun beams
in every drop

of rain
an arc

a curved
wet handle

of an anchor—
a rainbow—

mooring us
in the faithfulness

of God.

7 3

Heritage

Craftsman are repairing
the Victorian tower
built in 1875:

six European stories
high, breasted
with capped angles,

curled wood, glazier's
art. Scaffolding
sheathes the sky

about the tower
like poplar boughs.
Above, planets

delicately trace
the circling air
banding the tower,

a bird to be saved
for its song;
an ikon,

cherished for wonder.

After Silence

Down the mountainside
cool spray of glacier water
falls into meadows of wild flowers.

From this faraway place, you send
love's improvident gift:
wild blue flax, yellow

cone flower, stiff-petalled
Indian blanket seeds. Disbelieving,
I sift them into moist soil.

Today, in the live universe
of a flower pot, silken leaves
spear upward: a fragment

of the day of creation.
The gift is so much the giver.
I bend to the frail green

like an amateur trying
to photograph butterflies
drinking from a stream.

The Suicide

Though he had longed
for the calm of water
when the car climbed
Bay Bridge, he was afraid.

He felt so alone.
He was the erring son.
No one he had ever tried
to love was near.

Midway on the bridge,
motor running, he thrust
at the door and
leaped the guard rail.

He hit the water
arms outspread
like Jesus sweating
on his face

in garden grass.
No one saw
ministering angels
under water.

Boy in a Museum

He is seven years old. Knee knobs
are angular pink, sturdy as sprockets.
He is warm in his school-yard jacket,
intense with effort—be quiet, be good.

He bellyflops on the cool museum floor,
opens the sketchbook, clutches the yellow
pencil in whose graphite point
millenia are gathering to his call.

He stares in the rib cage of a "giant
deer in Ireland 11,000-12,000 years
ago" trellises of bone, spinal cord
delicate as fern, empty brain cage

levering no wind at all. His eyes
touch the unseen pelage, the lemming
and hare that bound away from the hooves.
He hears the file of deer

emerge from the tree line, springing
toward the reindeer moss where he lies.
It is two o'clock of any school day,
and whom will he tell

of the falcon swooping down
the roof, the saddle of hills
he has climbed that day, the snowmelt
he has trudged, the eons he has lived.

Making a Terrarium

Metallic leaves
lock about
my fingers
like membrane
to my mouth.

I cup
black earth
in hand
(roots tremble
at the push
of air)
funnel fingers
into the bowl,
slip soil
on pebbles,
tamp roots
into wet earth,
unlock leaves,
slide the glass
roof over
a simple world:
air   light   water
earth greening
toward spring,
repeat creation's
(God as human)
it is good.

At the Beginning

The first real snow came late, in March.
Through the night, updrafts of whiteness
billowed, settled, crusted, packed.
In the morning, small boys came

to this special place: behind old stables,
a hill of snow floating to a hockey field.
They had no sleds, trays, not even
cardboard. It'd been long

since they had snow. They raced the slope,
dolphin-poised, came down head first,
zippered windbreakers lunging into snow,
faces burning cold.

Intense, and caring,
they prophesied the moment
when, each in his hour,
would be taken by love.

Back Porch Fundamentalist

In the afternoon
he chose the corner in the sun.
Then he set his porch rocker
facing the mimosa
where gold wires
of light tapped
the leaves, and he, himself,
by a simple act of seeing
observed a miracle.
If anything is, he said,
them pods
on this tree is the keys
of the kingdom.

Night Walk: Kyoto

In fields of rice
moonlight shines on still water,
frogs are wakening;
we listen to the sound that
Aristophanes heard.

Moss Garden

Saijo-zenji, Kyoto, Japan

Moss is what it is.
A drop of dew
and miniscule kingdoms

rise and send out
envoys of hope: to
forests and flowers,

fairy cups and cushions,
flowerless plants and fruit
on rock, tree,

damp earth
along a luminous pond,
beside a stream,

on bridges of log,
small stones.
Moss holds the rain.

Moss is what it is.
jade? emerald?
light shining from eons.

God takes flesh
this way
or that

shows himself
hiddenly
as here he is

impossibly possible
in this garden.
Moss holds the rain.

Intuition

I took this journey to redeem
a lackluster sabbatical.
In Athens, fled the tourists and the guide,
visited cave churches in Cappadocia
and Istanbul.

Sometimes, I walked in valleys
of wild thyme and mint, glimpsed a golden
oriole. In taverns where I stayed,
woke at dawn as though I sailed on lakes
of mist low-lying between houses moored
to pitted olive trees and cypress plumes.

Briefly, women at wine presses smiled
at me. In the sun, they seemed to wear
long gloves of drunken wasps falling
into wine. Their faces were soft
as olive oil.

Finally, I sailed to Ephesus.
It was spring. Pilgrim muslims
stepped between anemone,
going softly.
> *Take your heart within your hands,*
> *the mother of the prophet Jesus*
> *wondered here.*

Had I come this far
to be home? knocking with my brothers
at the door of peace?

O *Maria.*

Summer Morning

Morning is no Moses,
wears no veil upon those
horns of light.

Past airy leaves
squirrels astronaut
in space;

white enamel
droppings shine
creaturely

of birds.
My own voice
cries silently,

echoing
from childhood
play:

Come out, come out,
wherever
you are.

And I
tremble
at a presence.

The Father

Luke 15:11-32

Never had the old man made such a journey.
His robes enfolded him like driving wind.
No one remembered the old man running. Even fire
had never moved him. His estates were the light
of the town. Yet, there he was, running to a dark
figure huddling the road. Love was flood-water

carrying him forward. Some tried to dike the water;
nothing could hold him. Love loosed a wind
of words: "My son is coming home." Dark
grief behind, the father ran, arms open as light.
He had to lift the boy before his son's fire
of sorrow burned the father's sandals. Journey?

The old man could remember no other journey
but this homecoming: he held his son in the fire
of his arms, remembering his birth: water
and fire. Servants ran along thrusting at the wind
of excitement: what shall we do? what torchlight
prepare? "Bathe away the pig-pen-slopping-dark

that cloaks my son. Prepare a banquet. Jewel the dark
with fires. My son was dead. My son is afire
with life. The land is fruitful. Joy is its water.
Where is my eldest son? The end of the journey
is ours. My son, do you grieve? turn from the light
to say you are unrewarded? Son, is the wind

from the south closer than you to me? is the wind
of your doubt stronger than my love for you? Water
your hardness, my son. Be a brother to the dark
of your brother's sorrow. Be a season of light
to his coming home. You will make many a journey
through cities, up mountains, over abysses of fire,

but for tonight and tomorrow, my eldest, fire
your heart, strike at its stone. Let it journey
toward dawning, be a thrust at the dark
your brother will never forget. Find a woman of water
and fire, seed her with sons for my name and wind-
supple daughters for bearing daughters and sons of light.

I am a father of journeys. I remind you the dark
can be conquered by love-blazing fire. I made air and wind
a compassionate homeland. Be at home in the light."

PART FOUR

Coming home to light

Someone You Love

When I see you coming home,
I am most like God who could
embrace the wholeness of the world:
It is good.

Parting

It was the day on which
he smiled, but did not take
an order for a bench;
listened, but did not make

an answer to his friends
who talked of John, said
perhaps he was the one
men waited for. His head

bent to the earth in prayer—.
More than before? Mary knew,
yet did not know. She saw
him bless the room, new

wonder in his eyes as
he asked her blessing, laced
his sandals, clasped his cloak
and simply left the place.

Then Mary was alone:
the end began with going.
The words she'd always kept
became that deeper knowing.

Thomas Jefferson at Seventy

Crippled wrists and fingers make
my writing slow. . . . And yet

I have a mockingbird I often take
from out its swinging cage. A pet?

I think of it as something more.
The strong feet grip my flesh:

down-curved, the bill explores
my hand. Gardeners bring fresh

seed for me. And then he sings.
That repertoire! My whole life—

a golden age of seeking—rings
in his galaxy of song. Pain? Strife?

Yes. But hope has steered my bark.
Men ride their fear in skiff or ark.

I take a mocking bird into my dark.

Ireland: A Selective Memory

i

the trip

In October, fog leans
against the land
like a wet dog.

On the west, wind blows
rain on the cliffs
of Moher, and around
our small car
nosing sheep
on the lonely road.

We long for the warmth
of a pub,
men talking
their histories.
    Easy
silence welcomes us.
We drink mugs
of listening.

ii

bed and breakfast

We stop anywhere
the B and B sign
creaks on a roadside

staff, or whistles
from a window.

In the bedroom
Jesus on the crucifix
hangs, ready to embrace
our sleeping.

Are there any
wrong choices
for B and B?

The choice we make
is always right:
bed-quilts whisper
to each other *warm warm.*
Hot tea
cups sleep
like a sigh.
Breakfast—thick brown bread
butter eggs sausage tea.
We eat the kitchen.
Kindness is honey.

iii

for the photo album

Whoever is not driving
takes what the light gives:
Knockmealdown mountains,
the monastery at Cashel,

Galway, Roscommon, Athlone,
Wicklow, Castlebar.

iv

In the parish house
the priest thumbs
old baptismal lists: Patrick,
Ellen, Nora, Brendan, Michael,
Sheila—may they rest in peace.

Four moss-covered steps
into the cemetery, we foot-
print the dust of our lives.

v

return home

If we retell stories
that we heard,
forgive us. All
the stories
are our own.

Summer

fills the white enamel bucket, overflows
its red rim with black-eyed susans.

Light has poured into
the brilliant petals hugging

purple-black, cone-shaped discs.
Hairy leaves, thick stems

gulp water in the bucket.
From a sunny meadow, I carry it

into the house pioneering backward:
decades ago, wagons from the west

loaded with hay and sweet clover
carried the seed of black-eyed susans

—the blessing on common things—from
Massachusetts to Georgia

so that Walt Whitman could say:
every hour of light and dark,

. . . every cubic inch of space
is a miracle.

From a Summer Diary

Only memory holds
that hummingbird,
too delicate

to be fossilized.
The female rubythroat
deposited her eggs

in a nest lined
with cushiony cobweb,
moss, fern fronds,

lichen, strands
of hair. Then I watched
78 wing beats

a second, less
than a penny
in weight.

Who lit
this wonder
for my eyes?

How can I speak
of God
except in the presence
of God?

The Physicist Gives Birth to Her First Child

Smiling,
the mother
looks down at the child
in her arm-cradle:
in how many ways
she has never known
light enters
a drop of dew.

Christmas

with a bowl of paperwhite narcissus

The cluster of flowers
follows an inner code
creating fragrant stars
taking position
in the galaxy of everyday.

So camel-tenders
and magi leaned back
on history
and the Persian sky
listening to a desert star
pull them toward
a Jewish child
with the face of God.

Eucharistic Minister

In the hospital room,
I light a candle,
lift the host, the Lord,
into your waiting hands.

And I eat the body
of Christ which you
with your suffering body
feed me.

Missionaries

Your feet, my sisters,
upon this mountain,
trace the power of God
signed upon the land.

You are the whorl
in the mountain's grain,
the knot of song
that holds the world.

Adjustment

Six meters high, the dinosaur rises
in the great hall of the Museum
of Natural History. Under its shadow
five college students re-create
a leviathan lizard with dragon teeth
(in wet plastic and papier-maché).

In the shadow of both
the first graders inhale
the unknown—staring up
until the dinosaur looks down.

Last Snow

Less alive than a Rockwell Kent scene
and more real: suburban afternoon hills
foundering in trampled snow and thin
interlocking up and down voices. Bells

of ice crystal ring from hemlock and pine
but the children do not hear.
They flop on sleds; gasp and keen
at runners blurring to spray; dare

the bounce between the hillocks; lunge
into crisp, sun-riddled banks. When dusk
clings to red soggy snow pants, and strange
six-rayed stars hang from mittens, they risk

"one more, just one more ride," before the long
pull home. Last elation fiercely cries
"tomorrow we'll come again, tomorrow we'll bring
the others." Their weighted bodies drowse

toward dreaming, while the south winds blow
rumoring the hills with morning thaw.

Spring Snow on Long Island

When my brother called
from Centerville
(ten minutes from Long Island Sound)
he skipped telephone amenities.
"We have mourning doves
nesting in the backyard maple tree."

"You had them before. Last summer?"

"We did. But this is March.
We're in a snow storm. I can't
believe it. The female warms
the flimsy nest. Snow comes down
like powdery cement.

I had to go to her. But
when I neared the tree, she flew up.
I saw—level with my eyes—two white eggs.

I backed into the house.
The mourning dove dropped to her nest.
Almost immediately, snow cloaked her.
She sat, unmoving. Snow outlined everything except that love song
coo coo I heard the male
singing weeks before."

"I can't believe it."

My brother stopped.
Wires sang silence.

I thought of Thomas, finger ready
to feel wet blood in Jesus' wound,
watching his dry finger in God's breath.

Friendship without End

He walks into the shabby room
gently. This world, too, will break
like a fever from the blackening tomb

of itself. He looks at his students.
Under the look, each man is alone,
astonished at the courtesy. "Who has condemned

you?—Neither will I." He serves
his students. A chair. A book. A glass
of water. The frailty of man deserves

redemption. He speaks—only a word,
a few words. Men gather the manna of
his praise. They have not often heard

themselves so reverenced. He
listens to them. Listening is a hand
on the shoulder, strength, mystery.

He turns their hearts to flesh. Grief,
fear, shriveling, loneliness, terror
are eased in the humility of his belief.

Such is the presence of a friend.
Such a presence does not end.

Litany for the Living

Hildegard of Bingen
Catherine of Genoa
Catherine of Sienna
Mechtild
Simone Weil
Edith Stein
Julian of Norwich
Teresa of Avila
Therese of Lisieux
Etty Hillesum
Marjorie Kempe
Mary Ward
our cloud
of witnesses
of flaming heart
light untouchable
dark immeasurable
mystic marriage
ground-of-being-God
the Father
God the Mother.

Writing Class: Senior Citizens

They are like photos sliding in frames.
They have come to the Center to talk, to write.
It is not easy. Where are the words? Times
they remember, they wear like a sprig

of sorrow. Years they knew simmer like soup
on the farthest burner. Take out a spoonful?
Gravely they listen to the woman who says: "Write
what you remember." The yellow pencil swollen

as their bones moves: "I had four
brother and eight sister. . . . My father
kill hogs and we wash them with pepper. . . .
We raise corn, beans, peas, greens. . . ."

The teacher reads back the words,
"Good. Good." They nod. They feel
under heart-arrest: a sagging rocking chair,
winter-chewed hedges, skinned squirrels,

chilblains, the grandmother, sand-scrubbed floors,
. . . where are the words? "The onliest
way to tell is to pick it—the way we pulled
blueberries when momma set us out with a pail

when I am the eleventh child in Carolina."

Eclogue and Elegy

Before the ants,
before the crows,
before the old hunting dog,
I found the bird.

The black mask
stared upward from the
olive gray head.

The yellow breast
shone in the sun.
The sound of *witchery witchery*
in marshy land, in tall grass,
stilled.

From the clear memory
of what I saw,
I speak a universal word.

Faith

Mark 5:35-41
Luke 8:22-25

Absurd, like a boy's,
that open, sleeping face.

How could he? in the stern?
what a place

for a pillow, a nap.
The boat groaned,

men clung to port,
starboard . . . moaned

in their guts.
Hostile water swept

them all toward death.
And Jesus slept.

They lived to tell
the tale: that face

asleep watching
like an oath. The grace

is to believe.
And so live.

Psalm from the Hemoglobin Ward

Yahweh, our brother lies helpless.
Terror swells a body
lumped with decay.

The hair of his head has fallen.
Sweat rises in sickening dew
from barren bone.

Light glows on the gourds
of his glands that declare
themselves grotesque.

Orderlies wait to lift him out
of the bag of VA hospital gown.
And his women wait,

wife and sisters, unable to speak,
crying in silence,
Yahweh—

the broken face of our brother
is the broken face of Christ:
ecce homo.

From a Woman's Life

What Mary knew was just
enough for the usual day:
pull water, flint fire, bake
bread, smile, pray

the dark orations, sleep, wake,
wait. When pain honed a nerve,
when birth or dying clotted
an hour, she leaned to the curve

of living, resilient to fear,
laughter, suffering.
Partings are a little death.
Each one's journey is a thing

wholly without precedent.
She looked at the sky
for compass. None. She, too,
created a road to travel by.

Easter Morning

We were not in a
place, though gnats
rising from wet grass

proclaimed their meadow.
We were not in a
time, though rafts of

light unmoored from the
eastern line of trees. We
were becoming, hearing

our hearts beat in a
rhythm impossibly possible:
60 trillion cells of every

human person affirming
not seeing is believing.

Out of Cana

John 2:1-11

The messenger came. The message was love
in a marriage feast. Would she come? grace
the young with her presence? help with the song
of her service? She began to walk to Cana. Life
on the road was busy: vendors of citrus and wine,
shepherds and sheep, and later, buoyance of dance

as the guests came into Cana. Sun-dance
too on the feasting, and Mary with deepening song
in her heart, chatting or watching the grace
of the dancers till her son came in, a life-
magnet pulling his friends along. Tender love
exchanged with glances. Then they lifted the wine

of convivial pledges: the groom, the bride, the wine
of their offspring. Time was a flowering dance
of feasting and stomping. Only the watchful love
of Mary's friend, the bride's mother, sensed the song
diminish as wine ran low. Mary moved with grace
to a servant: "Fill the water jars." "With—?" "Life."

She smiled. "Whatever he says, do it, as though your life
hung on the words of my Jesus." He did. And a grace
went out from Jesus pouring into the water-wine
Yahweh's joy. The feast renewed. The dance
danced the miracle. The mother sang her song
again: Magnificat. And Jesus poured the Father's love

in touch, in word, in wine. Marriage-love
enwrapped the groom, the bride. With sleepy grace
guests walked home singing. One more glass of wine
the friends of Jesus said. And Jesus smiled a dance
of knowing at his mother. She held his life
as kairos-gift, parting, pain, fulfilling song.

Eat bread. Drink wine. Try to sing the song
of Christ. Live life. If you can dance, dance.
Everywhere grace awaits. Desire to love to love.

Handwriting on the Wall of Today

Crows black as printer's ink
a wren like a little finger
the drying butterfly pulling at sun
small leaves chiming clapperless bells
loosed from a larval envelope
a jewel of song and a dragonfly:
Just a few words in my father's hand.

After the El Greco Exhibit

They were exhilarated with the elegant
sobriety of Spanish dons; tapering
hands and elongated heads;

saints and Mary poised like
leaping fires of salmon, opaline-
pink, cinnamon, blue-green of

juniper berries caracoling on
a rock horizon. At a stop light
on the parkway, someone glanced

at a suburban lawn. Flirting with
the fading light, a goldfinch—
like a rabbit from a silken hat—

rose to the topmost branch
of a sycamore, flight feathers
overlapping filaments, downy

feathers air-trapping song.
This other gift.